Remembering
Jersey Shore

Joe Czachowski

TURNER
PUBLISHING COMPANY

Barnegat Light and lighthouse can be seen from Barnegat Bay and the Atlantic. Barnegat Bay is nearly 40 miles of estuary fed by many rivers and is linked to the Atlantic by the Barnegat Inlet. The light-keeper's house in front is gone and the lighthouse has physically been moved back a few times because of beach erosion. It is a beloved structure for South Jerseyans.

Remembering
Jersey Shore

Turner Publishing Company
4507 Charlotte Avenue • Suite 100
Nashville, Tennessee 37209
(615) 255-2665

Remembering Jersey Shore

www.turnerpublishing.com

Copyright © 2010 Turner Publishing Company

Library of Congress Control Number: 2010924316

ISBN: 978-1-59652-659-4

Printed in the United States of America

ISBN-13: 978-1-68336-843-4 (pbk)

CONTENTS

On Governor's Day, the governor and his constituents could enjoy a day at the beach. This photograph was taken on Governor's Day, 1925, at Sea Girt, the summer residence for the state's chief executive. The summer residence has since been moved to Island Beach State Park, farther south, in a more secluded but wildly beautiful setting.

Acknowledgments

This volume, *Remembering Jersey Shore,* is the result of the cooperation and efforts of many individuals, organizations, and corporations. It is with great thanks that we acknowledge the valuable contribution of the following for their generous support:

Gateway NRA/NPS
Library of Congress
Monmouth County Historical Association Library & Archives
National Archives
NAS Wildwood Aviation Museum
New Jersey State Archives; Department of State
www.moorlyn.com

We would also like to thank the following individuals for valuable contributions and assistance in making this work possible:

Jim Laymon, www.moorlyn.com
Joanne M. Nestor, Principal Photographer, New Jersey State Archives

In working on this book, my late wife, Patti-Ann, was constantly on my mind. She lost a courageous forty-seven-year battle against cystic fibrosis in 2000. There was no one I ever met who loved the Jersey Shore more than she did. I thank her for my inspiration.

— *Joe Czachowski*

_____

The goal in publishing this work is to provide broader access to a set of extraordinary photographs. The aim is to inspire, provide perspective, and evoke insight. In addition, the book seeks to preserve the past with respect and reverence. With the exception of cropping where necessary and touching up imperfections wrought by time, no changes to the photographs have been made. The focus and clarity of many images is limited to the technology of the day and the skill of the photographer who captured them.

— *Todd Bottorff, Publisher*

PREFACE

When you grow up in New Jersey, it's not a given that you are a Shore lover. There may even be some people who have only been there once in their lives. I was a little ambivalent myself for sixteen years, until one magic, sultry night in Seaside Heights during August of 1969. I was with a buddy on the boardwalk and saw a sign on the Chatterbox Bar advertising an appearance by the great Jackie Wilson. Jackie had been around for a while already, and I was into rock music, but I loved listening to my older brother's records of him. You couldn't touch that voice.

We were about six dollars and six years short of gaining entry, so we sat next to an exit and just listened. The set finished about 2:00 AM and we were nearly clobbered by someone opening the door to take out garbage. Just after that, out the front door came Wilson himself with a small entourage. I nudged my friend hard, pointed, and said, "Hey, it's Jackie Wilson." Jackie heard me, waved back, pointed at me and said, "Hey, man." I'd like to say it was sparkling sand, or the azure blue of the ocean, or the constant rhythmic crashing of the waves that captured me, but it wasn't any of that—it was Jackie Wilson. I never saw him again, but that night is one of my treasured memories and is the reason I returned to the shore year after year, until empty pockets forced me to work summers. Imagine that, working in the summer. Go figure.

When I was asked to write the text for this book project, I honestly figured writing a book about the Jersey Shore would be a "piece of cake." It wasn't. So much beauty, so few pages. I've learned to love the shore in all four seasons. The beach can be as beautiful on New Year's Day as it is on the Fourth of July. In September, when crowds are gone and the water's still warm enough for swimming, it's great. Going in the spring and sniffing salt air for the first time after a long winter makes your mouth water for summer. I discovered a lot about the history of towns I had been going to for years. For instance, I had been to Long Branch many times, yet I had never seen its Broadway, the main street, until I researched pictures of the town. I knew about Jersey's Revolutionary War history because I teach it, but I knew nothing about the rich history of so many of the towns that punctuate the coastline.

The Shore has a fascinating history: towns with names like Belmar, Avon-by-the-Sea, and Avalon; Native American influences, with rivers called Metedeconk and Manasquan and a bay called Absecon. There are 127 miles of beaches in the state. Along the stretch from Sandy Hook to Cape May Point there are no less than 51 towns to visit. All have charm, some have glitz, some have kitsch, but all have something that permeates your soul and makes you go back year after year.

Parallel to the Atlantic Ocean is the bay shore region. Barnegat Bay, Sandy Hook Bay, and the Great Bay are parts of the Shore but have a life separate from the sea. Thriving communities have sprung up and have become as important to the recreational aspect of the tourism industry as the beaches. The communities, too, can be at opposite ends of the spectrum. The rich mansions of Deal and Mantoloking are a stark contrast to the poverty of Asbury and the sections of Atlantic City beyond the casino shadow.

There is both a need for and a dread of tourist dollars along the Shore. On Memorial Day weekend, towns explode with excitement that rarely stops until Labor Day. Thousands more residents, from senior citizens to young condominium buyers, settle full-time in the area. "Day trippers" and short-stays—weekend to two-week renters—pack the bungalows and rental houses, clogging roads and stores, and raising the ire of the resident population. A derogatory term of unknown origin, "bennie," was given to those who change into their bathing suits out of their car trunk. The term is still in use, but summer traffic pays the freight.

The Jersey Shore continues to mesmerize people of all ages, yet some have taken the area for granted and put it into ecological peril. Environmental groups are at odds with developers. Mother Nature constantly steps in and warns both of the fragility of the coastline. It will never be as pristine as it once was, but there is still time to keep it safe. I hope you enjoy perusing this text and seeing the evolution of communities and the growth of the state along its border with the mighty Atlantic.

— *Joe Czachowski*

A crowded Atlantic City beach in the early 1900s could have unexpected diversions. This young lady is having her fortune told—or is her fortune-teller hoping to get a date for later in the evening?

PROFESSIONALS, PRESIDENTS, AND PIERS

(1800s–1905)

In the late nineteenth century, games between formally attired, refined couples were a leisurely yet elegant way to spend a sunny afternoon at Mr. McCrary's Cottage in Cape May.

This photo taken in the late 1890s shows horse-drawn carriages ferrying people from vacation quarters like this one, the Cape May Ocean House, to enjoy nearby activities. This style house is typical of many in the resort towns, catering to visitors from not only New Jersey but from the New York and Philadelphia areas as well.

The easiest—if not the only—access to most shore areas was by railroad. Many short-haul trains were in use in the late 1890s to early 1900s to transport passengers from water ferry stops to their destinations. You can see there is no separate tender for fuel, only the expanded cab. Apart from vacationers, the Shore was also a destination for military men and munitions manufacturers, coming to the Sandy Hook Proving Grounds where new weapons and ammunition were tested.

This photo from the early 1900s shows one of the New Jersey Central Railroad ferries that transported passengers to and from New York City to Sandy Hook, New Jersey. The image contains an interesting contrast in the changing modes of transportation, engine versus wind power, old versus new.

This early 1900s photo shows the bridge linking Atlantic Highlands with Sandy Hook, across the Shrewsbury River. You could have your photo taken for 50 cents with the Highlands Twin Lights as a backdrop. Built in 1828, the Twin Lights were the first to use Fresnel lenses and, later, electricity. Built to be a beacon for New York Harbor, the lights became a historic site in 1960.

"The life boat, my boys, is the best boat that floats," was the original caption on this Atlantic City image from around 1896. Many would agree, from distressed swimmers to storm and shipwreck victims. Lifeboat stations were part of the Jersey shoreline.

When this photograph was taken in 1899, crowds had already been flocking to Atlantic City for many years to saunter on the boardwalk and enjoy the sand and surf. This shows much of what they came for: the beach, the sea, fishing, and the many attractions—or should we say distractions?

The original Iron Pier on Decatur Street in Cape May from the early 1890s, crossing some salt marshes to reach the beach. It was probably ahead of its time; while it might suffer sea salt corrosion, it wouldn't burn. Fire would be a constant danger to so many of the shore boardwalks for decades to come.

The Hotel Manchester, Ocean Grove, taken in 1895. It has the Victorian "gingerbread" lattice work found in many of the Shore's towns. Ocean Grove was founded in 1869 as the Ocean Grove Meeting Association, a Methodist summer community. It remained a Camp Meeting Town until 1981. Two of the town's idiosyncrasies were: (1) no cars permitted on Sunday, which lasted until the 1980s; and (2) no alcoholic beverages permitted anytime, a real anomaly for a beach resort.

Boys of Captain Vredenburgh's Company, Seventh Regiment, are leaving from Penn Station Freehold for the Sea Girt Army Training Center on May 2, 1898. Sea Girt housed the State Militia Camp. These were preparations for the Spanish-American War.

One way of documenting your stay in Atlantic City in 1899 was to have your picture taken with the donkey wearing the "I could stay in Atlantic City forever" sign. The picture would be a cherished item for many.

On the Atlantic City boardwalk, 1902. People came to the shore for the supposed health benefits of the salt water. If you didn't want sand in your shoes or between your toes, the overlook on Richard's Baths was the way to go.

Exotic rides were among the varied attractions on the Atlantic City boardwalk. In this early 1900s photo, a couple is looping the loop. Not nearly as complicated as modern-day thrill rides, this still must have been exciting.

These two Atlantic City bathing beauties from around 1903 didn't need sunscreen. In the background is the double-decker pier from which visitors could watch the fun.

Asbury Park was located closer to the metropolitan area and became a popular destination. This early 1900s photo shows a typical crowd enjoying the water and watching others do the same. Little boys (foreground) have always loved to dig holes in the sand. I was always told China was at the other end.

An Asbury Park photo from around 1904 shows the contrasts of flashy attractions and elegant grandeur, with the Ferris wheel to the left, the large hotels lining the streets, and the flower beds surrounding a historical monument.

The newly constructed pier provides a seagull's-eye view of the splendid beach at Wildwood. Flags show the stiff breezes off the ocean. Hotels are right on the water in this photo from about 1905.

A crowd gathers at the corner of Ocean Avenue in Long Branch as shown in this 1905 photograph. The ocean wasn't the only attraction. Entertainment could vary at the shore from lectures to political speeches to musical concerts.

On the Atlantic City boardwalk in 1904, visitors had a variety of entertainment to choose from. The marquee beyond the wheeled chairs announces controversial actress and feminist Cecil Spooner is touring in the play *The Taming of Helen*.

The wide Asbury Park boardwalk pictured here around 1905 invited visitors to walk for entertainment, as many did. Amusements weren't added until later. The other thing to do was to fish. In the background, piers constructed for that purpose are visible.

This 1908 Ocean City photograph shows the advent of boardwalk stores. Some sold food, while shops like Frost Brothers offered useful beach items and city-like window shopping to make a sunny walk more interesting.

Growth and Destruction

(1906–1929)

The grandeur of the age and the area is depicted in Captain Young's House in Atlantic City around 1910. If one had money, one flaunted it. Built on what was known as the "Million Dollar Pier," the house was as spectacular as the view it commanded.

This early 1900s photo shows a crowded beach and surf in front of the Atlantic City Auditorium. With a seating capacity of 40,000, the auditorium hosted many large events of the day. Later, in the 1920s, it housed a pipe organ touted as the largest in the world.

Ocean City in the early 1900s offered a choice of entertainments. This photo shows the marquees of the Hippodrome, Strand, and (from the rear) Moorlyn theaters, along with Shriver's ice cream stand, reportedly the oldest business on Ocean City's boardwalk.

This bird's-eye view of the Atlantic City beach and fishing pier was recorded in July 1909.

Guests rest on the Grand Piazza of the Hotel Cape May around 1909. They could pass the hours relaxing, reading, or conversing while cool ocean breezes wafted through the spacious openings. This was the height of charm and elegance of the day.

This 1909 photo shows the Cape May Glass Company during the noon lunch break. Glassworks were a thriving business at the turn of the century. The area was certainly not lacking in a primary ingredient for glassmaking, sand.

This photo of the night shift at the Hereford Glass Works, Cape May, taken November 19, 1909, shows teenagers—and younger children—who earned a living in factories before the Progressive era of child labor laws and mandatory free public education. Even after those acts were passed, many youngsters lied about their age to inspectors, in order to continue bringing money into their households.

This must have been a gorgeous weekend day; at such times, crowds were constant. This is the Atlantic City boardwalk around 1910.

We can only imagine what it must have been like for Atlantic City residents who first saw men flying above them. These three biplanes circled above the boardwalk area around 1910.

Wheeled chairs that allowed ladies to traverse the boardwalk in shaded comfort had become part of the scene years before this picture was taken around 1910. In the background is the Hotel Traymore, a majestic structure with finely manicured grounds in the front.

A photograph of St. Catharine's Church in Spring Lake around 1911. All religious denominations were represented in the Shore communities. While serving year-round congregations, religious institutions welcomed visitors in the summer months. One couldn't ignore Sabbath duties just because one was on vacation.

Special boardwalk events were created to swell the already large crowds. Here in 1915 on the Asbury Park boardwalk, is one of the more popular—the baby parade. Both infant and carriage would be adorned for the occasion. As is apparent by the number of onlookers, people enjoyed the spectacle.

"Votes for women" activists had a busy summer in 1915. These three suffragists are putting up a poster advertising a speech by activist Anna Howard Shaw, whose biography, *The Story of a Pioneer,* was published that year. Suffragists took advantage of the summer weather and the crowds from Keyport to Atlantic Highlands to Asbury Park to stage events such as concerts, lectures, parades, and even ball games. Famed activist Alice Paul was born in Burlington.

The Cape May Lighthouse, built in 1859, still majestically adorns this southernmost point in New Jersey, where the Atlantic meets the Delaware Bay. It is still active, and the house to the right is still standing. In an agreement that benefits all, the Coast Guard leases the structure and grounds to the state, which in turn sub-leases it to the Mid-Atlantic Center for the Arts. All proceeds go for restoration and upkeep.

Former New Jersey governor Woodrow Wilson (1910-12) delivered his presidential nomination acceptance speech in September 1916 at Shadow Lawn in Long Branch. Shadow Lawn served as his summer White House upon his election to the presidency in 1912. It burned some ten years later, was rebuilt as the Woodrow Wilson House, and still serves an active role as part of Monmouth University.

Here are doughboys (a generic term for World War I–era soldiers) in training at the Sea Girt Militia training site in the summer of 1915. While Fort Dix is more closely associated with New Jersey military training, both the National Guard (militia) Center at Sea Girt and the Ordnance Proving Ground at Sandy Hook also provided it.

Damage from a December 26, 1913, storm. This photograph was taken in Seabright, just past Sandy Hook to the south. Seabright bore the brunt of many storms, which eventually led to the building of a huge seawall to protect the town. The trade-off for safety was massive beach erosion over time, which was not remedied until the late twentieth century.

The broad and lengthy boardwalks lent themselves to carnival parades. This one was in Long Branch in 1911. Now known as Macy's, Bamberger's was an extremely successful chain in New Jersey, headquartered in Newark. As populations moved to South Jersey, so did the enterprise, locating to centrally located shore towns. As advertised, it was the "always busy store."

The General Ulysses S. Grant Cottage was on Ocean Avenue in Long Branch. Grant spent much of the summer there in his "Summer White House" during his presidency (1869-77). He was the first president to discover the comforts of the area. The house was a gift to him from the town. It is said he enjoyed sitting on the back porch, smoking cigars and meditating, and he disliked interruptions. The house no longer stands.

This is the lavish Hotel Traymore, Atlantic City around 1920. Grand structures such as this were fairly standard in the day, to attract upscale clientele. What more could one ask for in this palace of luxury?

Margaret Gorman, Miss America 1922, stands surrounded by young girls in dancing costumes on the boardwalk in Atlantic City. For many, many years Atlantic City was synonymous with the Miss America Pageant, but in recent years the pageant has chosen to move elsewhere. If Bert Parks, who was the longtime host of the affair, no longer croons his famous "There she is, Miss America," maybe it was time to go.

King Neptune (Hudson Maxim) proclaims Margaret Gorman Miss America on September 7, 1922. There was a carnival and parade given during the weekend festivities. The pageant was traditionally held over the Labor Day weekend.

A charter fishing boat is headed out of the Cape May yacht basin for a day on the ocean. Esso gas and oil, on the right, was a trade name adopted in 1929 by Standard American Petroleum Company, one of the Standard Oil affiliates. "Esso" was the phonetic spelling of SO (short for Standard Oil). Today, we know it as Exxon.

Fishing was not just sport but a livelihood in many small, inland shore communities. Here the net haul of the day is being taken off a commercial boat to be separated before being sent to market. The crew works under the eyes of curious onlookers.

The popular Freemason organization had this grand temple built in Atlantic City.

ATLANTIC CITY N.J. BEAUTY PAGEANT

Crowds throng the Miss America Pageant in Atlantic City. The city probably could have survived without it, given the many attractions there, but this annual end-of-summer ritual was a boon, creating much larger than usual attendance late in the season.

Four bathing beauties in a September 8, 1922, photo from Atlantic City wore outfits that would have been considered "scandalous" just a few years earlier. These young women may have been contestants in the Miss America pageant, or perhaps they were simply discussing their merits compared to those of the contestants.

This 1925 view from the Hotel Traymore in Atlantic City shows what is most likely a weekday, given the small crowds. A sailor, home from the sea, strolls with friends. You can notice the expansive pier in the background and the Camel advertisement.

How to resist waffles and doughnuts on vacation, especially at those prices? The Creole was located on the Ocean City boardwalk. It burned in 1927.

Flags fly in a stiff ocean breeze at Atlantic City in this 1924 photo. A typical day, with the cabana chairs lined up and the pier with rides and amusements in the background.

The New Stockton Villa on Ocean Avenue in Cape May around 1925. The New Stockton was typical of many such houses constructed at the time. They were usually built a block or two from the beach for easy access.

President James A. Garfield was another of seven American presidents to get a respite from his workload at the Jersey Shore, specifically in Long Branch. Like President Grant before him, Garfield used a cottage in summer months. When he was struck by an assassin's bullet, he was brought there in the hope sea air would aid his recovery. He died there September 19, 1881. The photograph shows the Garfield Cottage in the 1920s.

On October 11, 1927, a fire destroyed nearly all of the Ocean City boardwalk between Moorlyn Terrace and 10th Street. This view at 9th Avenue was taken the day after. Shriver's Salt Water Taffy and the Hippodrome Pier were among the victims. This consuming blaze is said to have started in a pile of trash under the boardwalk. The strong wind off the ocean caused structures to burn all the way to the ground.

Shore towns are not just for summer tourists. They are thriving, year-round communities. One example of this is the beautifully planned Atlantic City High School Plaza from 1928. In the foreground in the circle is the Soldier's Memorial. At the rear right, at the end of the street is the World War I Monument and at the rear, Atlantic City High School.

For those taking a ride on the Reading or Pennsylvania Railroad, departure was from the Atlantic City Union Station. This photograph is from around 1928.

What the best-dressed Shore man would wear—such as Adam's Hats or spiffy white shoes—could be purchased at places like Barton's Men's Shop in Belmar. This is not a boardwalk store. Most of the larger Shore towns had a business district separate from the businesses along the ocean. When this photo was taken in the 1920s, automobile drivers still needed signs like the one on the pole to remind them, "Move on green only."

Moving day for this tourist attraction came the year after the 1927 Ocean City fire. With much effort, the Music Pavilion building is being turned 90 degrees and moved backward up to 6th Street, to accommodate the new, larger boardwalk which would account for more people and consequently, more revenue.

This well-detailed sand fort was constructed in 1926 by five industrious lads to guard the shores at Beach Haven. The squad has their tattered American flag flying proudly. Cannon is manned and ready as the "commander" in his sailor suit looks out for the enemy.

A fantastic aerial view of the famed Atlantic City Steel Pier in 1929. There was so much to see and do: Ronald Coleman's first talking picture—the first Bulldog Drummond film with sound—a minstrel opera, a water sports carnival, and the Steel Pier Revue with a high-diving horse and a Hawaiian village. There is also excellent signage for Texaco, General Motors, and Ethyl gasoline. In its heyday, the Steel Pier was one of "the" destinations.

The remains of the Colorado Hotel in Belmar after a fire in October 1922. The Colorado spanned an entire block between 14th and 15th avenues.

The Children's Seashore House for Invalid Children in the mid-1920s. Established in 1872, it was a rehabilitation and convalescence hospital for children with chronic illnesses, founded by Dr. William Bennett. It was one of the oldest pediatric institutions in the country. This building closed in 1990 when the hospital moved to Philadelphia.

New Dangers and a New Deal

(1930–1949)

Ventnor City is more or less a suburb of Atlantic City. Founded in 1889, like many other communities, it wanted an identity of its own. Named after a city in England, it officially went from Ventnor to Ventnor City in 1903. This photograph of the city hall is from the early 1930s.

This is the Burlington Library on West Union Street, Burlington, in March 1937. It is New Jersey's oldest library in continuous operation, established in 1757. Nearly half of Burlington County lies between Atlantic and Ocean counties. All three counties make up a large part of the rich agricultural areas of the Garden State. The most popular crops grown there are blueberries and cranberries.

The Cape May boardwalk in the 1930s. Constitution Hall is in the center of the buildings on the left.

The German airship *Hindenburg* resting at its moorings during a visit to the Lakehurst Naval Air Station in Lakehurst, possibly in May 1936. At a height of 803.8 feet and a diameter of 135.1 feet, she was the largest airship ever built. A symbol of Nazi power with the swastika emblazoned on the tail section, the ship mysteriously burst into flames as it landed on a return trip to Lakehurst, May 6, 1937, and was destroyed. Herbert Morrison's famous eyewitness account was broadcast over the radio with the heart-wrenching phrase, "Oh the humanity."

Salt marsh hay was harvested and marshland drained to be converted to agricultural use; this may also have been a mosquito-control measure. This photograph shows man and machine clearing a field in Atlantic County in the mid-1930s. Salt marsh hay was used as weed-free mulch.

A field worker sits on a scoop putting on her gear for a day of harvesting cranberries. The effort was labor-intensive in the mid-1930s, before widespread reliance on mechanical harvesters and harvests using water, which has been used for many years to flood the fields and float ripe berries to the surface.

In this mid-1930s photo, Elizabeth White is tending to a machine invented by her father, J. J. White, to sort cranberries. J. J. White founded the town of Whitesbog and turned his attention to blueberries. He and his daughter worked diligently to cultivate and expand blueberry production and promote the tiny fruit as an important and tasty dietary ingredient. It became the New Jersey state fruit.

Here is the face of immigrant labor in the 1930s. Puerto Rican laborers Pedro Novaro and Juan Ortiz wear the badges that authorize them to pick fruit. The Garden State Farmers Association arbitrated agreements between itself and fruit growers. Grower Tom Battaglia signs the contract held by Joe Garafolo, placement officer for the association.

The Bivalve oyster fleet is waiting around 1933 for nets to be loaded onboard, in order to start out for a full day's work.

Nets shown are those used for dredging the bottom for shellfish. Here in 1933 they are hung up to dry for the next trip. Bivalve is in Cumberland County along the Delaware Bay. The Maurice River feeds into the Delaware near there, and the area was a mainstay of the shellfish industry.

Clearing the cranberry bogs was not easy work. Cranberries were a true cash crop in New Jersey, harvested in Burlington, Atlantic, Cape May, and Cumberland counties. All these coastal counties had the marshland area to support cultivation. The photograph is from the mid-1930s.

A mid-1930s photograph of Ocean Avenue, Long Branch, shows a busy summer day among the food stands, tackle shop, and amusements. A man patiently waits to cross the street. It must have been a simpler time—no parking meters to feed.

The windmill-style building on the right was a Western Union tower used to carry wireless messages across long distances. It was located on Sandy Hook. Another tower is being added and the construction is following more conventional "lighthouse" design. These harbingers of expanding technology were probably photographed in the early 1930s.

Two members of the Grove Tuna Club are shown here hard at fun. The mate gaffs the prize of a long struggle. Tuna are an exciting game fish to grapple with and the waters off New Jersey have always been a fruitful spot for yellowfin, bluefin, and bonito.

In Cape May, the Colonial Hotel blended the Victorian with a more modern style, more for function than decoration. It worked, and these types of hotels became popular. The buildings had it all, large porches on which to relax, immaculate grounds, and spacious dining rooms. The street sign identifies a bus stop.

This is the Bivalve oyster dock shipping platform. The daily catch came in one side and went out the other on the same day, loaded onto railroad boxcars. There was a lot of competition, as evidenced by all the company signs.

A pleasant day on the Asbury Park boardwalk in 1932. Asbury was developed in 1887, named for Bishop Francis Asbury of the Methodist Episcopal Church. The concept was to have a "country by the sea." It flourished in the 1920s with its Beaux Art building design. At the end of the boardwalk is the Casino Complex—not a casino in the gambling sense, but one which housed amusements.

A photo of the Old Burnell House on Beesley's Point in Cape May County, taken August 13, 1938, shows a simple, plain, functional style, representative of the people who inhabited the lower New Jersey counties.

This Easter time 1938 photograph shows the corner of Atlantic City's Steel Pier. Crowds file past the imposing signage advertising "all for one admission." Imagine seeing great period stars like Deanna Durbin, Leslie Howard, and zany bandleader Kay Kyser, as well as two orchestras, two pictures, a game room, big exhibits, and more. As the sign reads, "Your stay in Atlantic City is not complete without a visit to the world famous steel pier."

A great posed photo, probably for advertising purposes, in the Sterling Cafe at Ocean City in the mid-1930s. Waitresses dressed in crisp, white uniforms served patrons. Unusual ceiling lamps, cozy wooden booths, and starched linen tablecloths complete the effect.

The Steel Pier in July 1938 advertising "A vacation in itself" and "Nowhere else can you see so much for so little money." The theater was also now air conditioned. Asbury Park native Bud Abbott and Patterson, New Jersey's Lou Costello joined other top acts like Benny Goodman's Big Band, Parisian dancer Danielle Darrieux, and Stooges Moe, Larry, and Curly Joe.

Salt water and air were considered conducive to healing. The Betty Bacharach Home for Crippled Children was located near a streetcar crossing in Atlantic County. It is now used as the Borough Hall for Longport, New Jersey, which was incorporated in 1898. The borough was formed from land in Egg Harbor Township.

The Old Cape May County Courthouse, built in 1825 and photographed around 1935, is designed in a simple, New England Meeting House style.

The 1938 hurricane and ensuing tidal wave caused this damage along the 10th Avenue section of the Belmar boardwalk. The boardwalk is always vulnerable.

A sightseeing plane and crew on the Shark River in Belmar, taken in 1938. They seem to be poised for a scenic late-summer flight.

This "colored church," photographed in the early 1930s, is the St. James A.M.E. Zion Church on Atlantic Avenue in Matawan. The church was organized by Richard Little and his daughter Matilda Conover in 1843.

The studio and broadcast towers of radio station WPG near the beach in Atlantic City are shown here in the early 1930s. The 5,000-watt station, operated by the Columbia Broadcast System, advertised Atlantic City as "the world's playground." Also shown are the tennis courts on Bader Field.

Either sail or motor power would provide an enjoyable day of sightseeing on the waters around Atlantic City in the 1930s. The sign in the background promotes an animal circus and water sports.

With all the horse farms in Monmouth County, racing and jumping weren't the only activities. A polo match is in progress in Long Branch in the mid-1930s. Long associated with the "upper class," playing polo harkened back to the early glory days of the Jersey Shore.

Seven hundred acres were set aside in 1932 to build what became Cheesequake State Park. Work began in 1938, using labor from the federal Works Progress Administration. The grant eventually grew to one thousand acres. Governor A. Harry Moore is pictured giving the dedication speech. Moore served three, nonconsecutive terms as governor from 1926 to 1941.

Broadway in Long Branch is bustling in the early 1940s. Long Branch was one of the larger shore area towns. This off-season image may show a Saturday, with cars lining the streets and people shopping for groceries at the Great Atlantic and Pacific Tea Company (commonly known as A&P) or for furniture at Sterenbuch's. There is even a corner cigar store.

Two of the top stars of the era star in a film at the Strand in Ocean City, July 1941. The salt water taffy sign beckons on the right. This traditional chewy souvenir candy does not list salt water as an ingredient. The legend is that David Bradley, an Atlantic City shop owner, had his taffy supply saturated with salt water during a storm. Enjoying its many flavors while taking in the salt air, makes for a memorable experience.

A good day at Cliffwood Beach in summer 1941. Cliffwood Beach is a small town, right where the bay-shore turns to meet the Atlantic. Relief from the sun could be sought beneath the pavilion—but please, don't undress on the beach.

Many clubs like the Colony Surf Club existed along the shore, providing a place to change clothes, enjoy a meal, and use the beach. Some had both freshwater and saltwater pools. There would be a fee, of course, and in keeping with the attitudes of the day, not all were open to the general public.

The Ventnor Boat Works wharf on Lake's Bay in Ventnor. This early 1940s photograph shows a docking facility and a house built upon a pier. Access to the Atlantic from here was through the Great Egg Harbor Inlet. Great Egg Harbor and Inlet and Little Egg Harbor and Inlet were so named because of the abundance of gull eggs found by early explorers and settlers.

100

A group photo of Long Branch's bravest from the early 1940s. Long Branch was a large town and needed dependable protection. A small group of full-time firemen were the first to respond to an emergency. They were supplemented by a dedicated volunteer force. In 1940, there were 9 full-timers; today there are 23.

This view down one of the hundreds of lagoons dotting the shore—this one in Ventnor—shows some residences with built-in boat houses. These lagoons have scores of boats, contributing to extensive recreation and commercial activity on bays, rivers, and the ocean.

A close-up look at the Long Branch Fire Department shows Independent Engine and Truck Company No. 2 on Third Avenue in the early 1940s.

A smokestack proudly bears the town name at the Ventnor Waterworks. An elaborate fountain adorns the front lawn. If it wasn't for the smokestack, one might mistake this for a stately manor. An ornate crest above the entrance memorializes the year it was constructed, 1923.

A view of Ventnor from a fishing pier. The small beach crowd probably indicates a weekday. This photo from the 1940s showing a very small beach area is a good illustration of how susceptible to extreme weather conditions shore communities can be. Imagine gale-force winds swallowing up the sand in very short time. Waves then demolish the boardwalk, sending pounding surf and wooden timbers directly into the houses.

After World War II began, many miles of coastline needed to be patroled, regardless of weather, and horses provided the best means of coastline transportation. Pictured left to right in 1942, these four members of the Coast Guard Beach Patrol are Seamen First Class C. R. Johnson, Jesse Willis, Joseph Washington, and Frank Garcia.

Preparing for war is hazardous business. This TBF torpedo bomber crashed west of the U.S. Naval Air Training Station at Wildwood in Cape May County in the early 1940s. Upward of three dozen men lost their lives in training accidents in the area during the war.

An early 1940s photo of the Long Branch Train Station on what appears to be a quiet day. The first set of tracks, running along the brick-paved street, is probably the original. Another, more modern set has been laid alongside.

The Monmouth Park Racetrack is one of the most attractive tracks in the United States. Originally opened in 1870, it closed several times due to financial difficulty. It reopened for good in 1946 when state regulations on the racing industry were enacted. It is a "flat" or thoroughbred race course. One of the annual events is named after a famous New Jersey Revolutionary War figure, The Molly Pitcher Breeders Cup Handicap.

This fisherman seems to have caught the evening meal. This perilous pier is not indicative of most of the shore fishing. Surfcasters have ample room to cast on the many beaches, but there are numerous rock jetties all along the coast where anglers can be a little safer than these two men.

This is the Ocean Grove Auditorium decorated to celebrate its 75th anniversary in 1944. Ocean Grove is a unique community. Founded by William B. Osborn in 1869 as a religious resort, it was famous for its summer religious camp meetings. Tents from those meetings eventually gave way to cottages and hotels. Still a vibrant community, it remains true to its mission and has an annual summer religious celebration.

Here are German prisoners of war working on mosquito control near the U.S. Naval Air Station in 1944. Though the Cape May–Wildwood area was well populated, the naval station had the military capacity to house and guard the POWs.

Progressive Party presidential candidate Henry Wallace speaks at a rally in Asbury Park on July 18, 1948. Wallace was vice-president under Franklin D. Roosevelt from 1941 to 1945. Despite Wallace's popularity at this event, Democratic candidate Harry Truman, his successor as Roosevelt's VP, ultimately won the election.

The calm after the storm. A damaged pier, a bent section of rail, numerous boardwalk planks strewn about, and not much beach area are left in the wake of a late-1940s storm. Boarded-up storefronts are the only protection from the elements.

Large and small charter-fishing craft wait for the next day's customers in Tom's River.

The Naval Chapel just outside the grounds of the Lakehurst Naval Air Station is also called the Cathedral of the Air. Ground was broken in 1932 for a place to memorialize the devotion of aviators to their service. It was built with the contributions and labor of the American Legion. Eighteen stained-glass windows have been added over the years to commemorate the history of flight.

The House of Israel Synagogue situated on a quiet street in Belmar, 1940s. The tranquillity belies the fact that the Jewish population had their share of problems within the community. The areas they settled at the Shore were given the derogatory name "bagel beach."

Atlantic City decorated for Christmas 1940. Lavish displays like this disappeared after December 7, 1941, but some stubborn Shore communities—like many others all along the East Coast—refused to completely darken their towns, perhaps for fear of a loss of revenue. This was much to the delight of German submarine commanders during World War II. The eastern American shoreline became the most dangerous passage for merchant shipping in the world until the federal government imposed mandatory blackouts in August 1942. Wartime censorship was also to blame; coastal residents were not told how bad the problem was.

BLUE-COLLAR PARADISE

(1950s)

McGuire Air Force Base is located in New Hanover Township approximately 45 minutes from Atlantic City. Originally established in 1937, it became an Air Force base in 1949 and is a vibrant part of the Burlington County economy. This late-1950s photo shows Miss Air Force in a parade on the Atlantic City boardwalk.

Getting ready for some sport fishing near the Barnegat Light in the mid-1950s, a fisherman checks the line on his surf pole. Striped bass, small bluefish, fluke, or flounder would be his likely catch. His Jeep has all the conveniences, plenty of rod holders, a cooler with refreshments, and a beach chair to relax in. There is nothing like it.

Republican governor Alfred A. Driscoll dedicates the Thomas A. Mathis Bridge in 1950, during the centennial of Ocean County. Mathis was a long-serving Republican state senator from the county. The bridge replaced a wooden structure across Barnegat Bay that connected Tom's River with Berkeley Township. Berkeley contains the beaches of Seaside Heights and Seaside Park.

The Berkeley-Carteret Hotel in Asbury Park was a grand symbol of Shore elegance. Built in 1924 and located on Ocean Avenue one block from the beach, it was named for the two original proprietors of the New Jersey Colony, Lord John Berkeley and Sir George Carteret. The hotel was the cornerstone of a once-vibrant city which has fallen upon hard times.

Here is a good example of the tranquil life at the Shore around the 1960s. Old and young enjoy the relaxation on Barnegat Bay. The solitary small boat suggests this is the off-season, early spring or fall.

Democratic candidate Adlai E. Stevenson spoke in Asbury Park during his run for the White House in 1952. He seemed to be a hit with this crowd, but he lost the election to Republican Dwight D. Eisenhower.

This elaborate complex is the Ventnor fishing pier and casino in the mid-1950s, a club providing members with access to the beach, along with other amenities. It would have been a restful place to enjoy the day. For a fee, you got access to the large fishing pier.

Long Branch Senior High School in the mid-1950s. A growing population was already putting pressure on Shore towns' infrastructure.

Pleasure craft are docked with people relaxing at the Cape May Marina, while a charter boat departs for some sport fishing. A longtime staple for the tourism industry and the local economies, charter-boat fleets operate from many marinas with easy access to the Atlantic. The job has become a family tradition, with boats passing from father to son to son. They go out for half and full days, afternoon and evenings.

Two men are working on the hull and transom of a boat at the Carver Boat Works in Bay Head. Boat building was an art for many along the bays and rivers of New Jersey. Skill and a dedication to the craft made it rewarding work. It remained so until the advent of fiberglass, a technology good for the boater, bad for the independent builder. A few of these craftsmen are still around in Jersey, but it is a dying art.

Many of the yacht clubs provided sailing instructions, teaching the ancient art. Here on the Shrewsbury River in Long Branch in the late 1950s, this might be graduation day, with a regatta to celebrate new-found water skills.

In the late 1950s in the town of Brielle on the Manasquan River, the Brielle Inn served fresh seafood dinners at the boat basin. Tasty fare for all seafood lovers of Jersey Shore communities.

Notes on the Photographs

These notes, listed by page number, attempt to include all aspects known of the photographs. Each of the photographs is identified by the page number, a title or description, photographer and collection, archive, and call or box number when applicable. Although every attempt was made to collect all data, in some cases complete data may have been unavailable due to the age and condition of some of the photographs and records.

Printed in the USA
CPSIA information can be obtained
at www.ICGtesting.com
JSHW072024140824
68134JS00042B/3778

9 781683 368434